Miracle Moments

Stories of God's Presence in Ordinary Life

GWEN EBNER

Path to Wholeness Publishing

Miracle Moments: Stories of God's Presence in Ordinary Life

Printed in the United States of America
ISBN 978-0-9981787-3-8

Formatted by Katie Erickson, KatieEricksonEditing.com.

I want to thank my two daughters, Shelley and Stacey for their loving help and care during my illness. Also, thanks to my husband Chet for the many times he has gone with me to oncology appointments and has helped me at home.

I am grateful for the many people who have prayed for me. God has answered their prayers.

To my Lord and Savior, who has been with me and carried me through my illness. He has encouraged me to help others, letting go of my fears, which helped me find hope and joy. Thank you, God, for your miracle healing and for filling my life with even more Miracle Moments.

Table of Contents

Introduction

God performs wonders that cannot be fathomed,
miracles that cannot be counted.
Job 5:9

After I turned seventy-five, I began experiencing severe pain in my back. I eventually required surgery, and during the procedure, the doctor noticed something unusual.

A week later, I went to the doctor's office. The nurse gently said, "Gwen, I'm sorry to tell you that you have multiple myeloma, a type of cancer. You will need to find a specialist to help you."

Many people were praying for me, and I was deeply grateful when a miracle took place in my life. The experience stirred something within me. I began thinking about miracles--especially those recorded in the Bible—and how God had always been present in both ordinary and extraordinary moments.

I remembered Lazarus, whom Jesus called out of the tomb after four days, restoring him to life (John 11). I thought about the Israelites trapped between Pharaoh's army and the Red Sea, but God made a way where there seemed to be none (Exodus 14). I reflected on Shadrach,

Meshach and Abednego who trusted God in a fiery furnace, and discovered they were not alone there. (Daniel 3)

And above all, the greatest miracle was the death and resurrection of Jesus Christ. Three days after his death, the tomb was empty. He had risen—bringing salvation and eternal life for all who trust in him.

As I reflected on these miracles, I began to recognize the many *Miracle Moments* God had woven throughout my life. Some were dramatic and others ordinary. But each one was a reminder of God's care and presence.

This book is a collection of those moments. As you read, I invite you to reflect on your own life as well. You may discover miracles you hadn't noticed before—times when God showed up, guided you, protected you, or carried you through.

My hope is that you will become not just a reader, but a participant—remembering the wonderful miracles God has done in your life as you trust Him for what lies ahead.

God, we trust you because You make a way and You work miracles.

CHAPTER 1

An Unexpected Escort

Out of difficulties grow Miracles
Jean de la Bruyere

I got married in June 1972 and a month later, turned twenty-two. We were poor newlyweds, carefully watching every dollar, renting a small upstairs garage apartment in an older, upscale neighborhood in Houston.

One day, hurrying home from an event, we chose a shortcut through a part of the city known to be dangerous. It seemed faster—but it did not turn out to be wise. Suddenly, our car sputtered and died. We checked the gas gauge. Gas was there. What could we do?

We had no cell phones back then, no mechanical knowledge and no nearby friends. So, we locked the car and began walking hand in hand toward home.

A knot began tightening in my stomach.

It was a long walk through a neighborhood known for trouble. My husband had just been paid and was carrying cash. My thoughts raced—robbery, violence, fear of not making it home safely. We were small in stature and no match for danger.

Five minutes into our walk, a tall, husky man came toward us on the sidewalk. Fear rose inside me and in that moment, I whispered a prayer to God. *"Lord, please protect us."*

When the man came within a few feet of us, something extraordinary happened. He suddenly stepped off the sidewalk into the street. He walked around us in a wide arc—as if an invisible barrier surrounded us—then stepped back onto the sidewalk and continued walking on his way.

I looked at my husband in amazement. We both knew something unusual had just happened.

A few minutes later, a police car pulled up beside us. The officer looked at us in disbelief. *"What in the world are you two doing, walking in this neighborhood?"*

We explained that our car had broken down several blocks away and we had no way to get help.

I will never forget his reply, *"I'm not normally allowed to let people ride in my patrol car, but I'll take you home. If I don't escort you out of this neighborhood, you probably won't make it."*

I have never been so grateful to sit in the back of a police car. When we arrived home safely, we thanked the officer for his gracious act of kindness, then called a tow truck to pick up our car.

God had answered a whispered prayer with unmistakable protection, sending us an Unexpected Escort. Thank You, Lord.

Ways God Helped Me in This Story

1. When I saw the man coming toward us on the sidewalk, I immediately prayed to God. Something amazing happened. Maybe, just maybe, there were angels who had formed a block around us.

2. In the book of Daniel (3:14-27), it didn't say Shadrach, Meshach, and Abednego had seen the Fourth Man in the fire with them, but the king had. My story was similar. The man coming toward us, may have seen an invisible box shielding us, but we didn't see it. Jesus was carrying us through our 'trial of fire' just as he did with Shadrach, Meshach, and Abednego.

3. God also brought a policeman to us when we needed him the most. I will always remember what he said, "If I don't escort you out of this neighborhood, you probably won't make it." God, thank you for this miracle that helped us make it.

Where fear surrounded us,
God made a way.

Scriptures that Connect with this Story

I sought the Lord, and he answered me,
he delivered me from all my fears.
(Psalm 34:4, NIV)

Then you called out to God in
your desperate condition;
he got you out in the nick of time.
(Psalm 107:13, Message)

The Lord is my light and my salvation,
so why should I be afraid?
The Lord is my fortress, protecting me
from danger, so why should I tremble?
(Psalm 27:1, NLT)

From My Story to Your Story

Here are some questions for you to answer:

1. As you read my story, what story from your own life came to mind? (Write it below)

2. How did God help you in your story?

3. What bible verse comes to mind when you think about your story?

A Simple Prayer

Lord, you have carried us
through situations that
we can't control.
Thank You for your
presence and your safety.
Amen.

Appendix Activities

Go to Appendix A and do the "Self-Reflection Tool"
to discover where you've been growing
and where you want to grow.

CHAPTER 2

Between Exits and Fear

A miracle is--God can do what only God can do
Ronald Dunn

In the mid-1970's, my husband and I were serving at a church in Florida. When God called us to a new ministry in Colorado, we packed up everything we owned, loaded our one-and-a-half-year-old daughter into the truck, and began the long drive west.

Traveling with our one-and-a-half-year-old daughter meant we moved slowly, stopping at hotels along the way to help our little one manage the long trip. Each mile carried us farther from what was familiar and closer to what God had prepared.

When we finally crossed into Colorado, we breathed a sigh of relief. Our destination felt close. But as we continued along interstate 70, that relief began to fade. It didn't take long, however, to realize that the towns were sparse, the land undeveloped, and the exits were few and far between.

More than once, we wondered what we would do if something went wrong with the truck.

Several miles later, we heard an odd sound from the engine. Almost immediately, we knew we needed to pull over. We barely made it to the shoulder before the truck came to a complete stop.

My thoughts raced. We were stranded in a remote area, and the next exit was very far away. We were completely alone. We had no way to call someone since it was 1976—long before cell phones.

My husband turned on the hazard lights and opened the hood, hoping someone would notice. I stayed inside the truck, holding our little girl close. I could feel my heart pounding. Fear whispered its questions:

How would we get help?

Would anyone stop?

Were we safe?

Fifteen minutes passed, though it felt much longer. Then, in the distance, an old, worn truck appeared. It slowed down. It pulled over. It stopped behind us.

A scruffy-looking man stepped out and walked toward my husband. I watched carefully, unsure what would happen next. He asked what had happened, and my husband explained that the truck had suddenly stopped running.

The man offered to take us to the next exit—but we would have to ride in the back of his truck.

We were out of options. Reluctantly, I climbed into the cargo bed and sat on the cold metal floor, holding my daughter tightly in my arms. The truck accelerated quickly down the highway.

The wind rushed past us. My heart raced faster.

Were we safe?

Would he really take us to the exit?

In that moment, I had nothing to hold onto but God. Quietly, from the depths of my heart, I prayed,

"God, please get us to the next exit, safe and sound!"

There was no guarantee—only trust.

Time seemed to stretch endlessly, but finally the truck slowed. An exit appeared. He pulled into a gas station.

Relief flooded my soul.

We were safe.

As I stepped down, holding my daughter, I felt the tension leave my body. God had answered my prayer.

My husband contacted U-Haul, but help would take time. I then called the church office. Once again, God provided. A church member came for us, welcomed us with kindness, and even prepared us a meal.

In the span of just a few hours, we had gone from fear to safety…from isolation to care…from uncertainty to peace.

God had been there the entire time. He had seen us on that lonely stretch of highway. He had carried us Between Exits and Fear.

What could have been danger became divine protection. What could have been despair became a testimony.

This was not coincidence.

This was God.

This was a Miracle.

Ways God Helped Me in This Story

1. A scruffy-looking man pulled up behind us. When we told him what had happened, he offered to take us to the next exit if we were willing to ride in the cargo bed of his truck. It was a vulnerable moment, but God carried us from fear to safety with someone we didn't even know.

2. It was going to take quite a while for the U-Haul staff to move our belongings into another truck. We called our church and someone came to pick us up. We were blessed with a wonderful meal, and I whispered, *"Thank you, God, for this relief."*

3. Traveling with our one-year-old daughter made everything more challenging. From the U-Haul to the cargo bed of a stranger's truck, God protected us and brought us safely to Denver.

This was not coincidence. This was God. In a vulnerable moment, He wrapped us in His protection. He carried us from fear to safety.

Scriptures that Connect with this Story

When I am afraid, I put my trust in you.
(Psalm 56:3, NIV)

God is our shelter and our strength.
When troubles seem near, God is nearer,
and He's ready to help.
(Psalm 46:1, Voice)

The Lord keeps you from all harm
and watches over your life.
The LORD keeps watch over you
as you come and go, both
now and forever.
(Psalm 121:7-8, NLT)

From My Story to Your Story

Here are some questions for you to answer:

1. As you read my story, what story from your own life came to mind? (Write it below)

2. How did God help you in your story?

3. What bible verse comes to mind when you think about your story?

A Simple Prayer

God you are the source of comfort
in all our troubles. We know
you are willing to help us,
uphold us and supply our needs.
Amen.

Appendix Activities

Go to Appendix B and choose a few ways for "Practicing the Presence of God." Choose one app in the first section. Then choose one or two in the second section, "Paying Attention to God's Presence."
Do these practices as often as you can.
Share what you are experiencing with a friend and/or with the group you are in.

CHAPTER 3

Take Them Both

Miracles come in moments.
Wayne Dyer

On New Year's Eve 1976, my husband and I celebrated at a friend's house. Just after midnight, we said goodbye and headed home.

At half-past midnight, our headlights were the only thing cutting through the darkness on the Denver freeway. A dark figure suddenly appeared in the middle of the lanes, stopping us in our tracks. As we drew closer, the panic in his movements made it clear: he was flagging us down.

My husband was anxious and wanted to go around him. But something tugged at me, an unshakeable need to see what had happened. My husband rolled down the window and the man was yelling, "Help me, please help me."

We pulled onto the shoulder immediately as he began to describe his discovery: a man and a woman thrown from a motorcycle, struggling in the ditch. We rushed to their side and realized they were both critically injured.

We waited by the ditch so the man could go get help, since we had no cell phones at this time. Being pregnant with my second child, the sight of blood made me so nauseated. I had to return to the car. I sat there in the dark, watching the scene unfold, feeling helpless until I remembered I wasn't helpless at all; I could pray.

The man found a phone and quickly told 911 how alarming the couple looked. The dispatcher decided to send an air ambulance to the location and they arrived. When the emergency personnel brought the couple out of the ditch, they decided only one of them--the woman--could ride in the helicopter. They would call an ambulance to pick up the man. I felt concern that if the man couldn't go, he might not make it. I decided to whisper a prayer, hoping they would change their mind.

They were almost ready to leave when the flight medic said, *"I think we should take them both, even if it is going to be crowded."* So, the pilot reluctantly said the man could also come. I felt a deep joy when I saw him being placed in the helicopter.

We headed home with a heavy heart for this couple. Two days later we found the story in the newspaper. The woman had died, but the man, the one they almost left behind, had survived.

I believe God used that flight medic to speak up and make room. Three simple words, 'Take Them Both,' meant the difference between life and death. Because of that decision, a man lived.

God still works miracles, even in the dark, on an ordinary road, through people willing to listen.

Ways God Helped Me in This Story

1. I believe God quietly prompted me to suggest that my husband roll down the window so we could hear what the man needed. Because we responded, we were able to help in several ways.

2. We stayed with the couple after finding the man on the freeway, who was getting help. God led us to this exact place at the right moment so we could be of help.

3. Although we were not the medics, I was grateful I could pray. I silently prayed that they would take the injured man in the helicopter. Soon after, the flight medic said, "I think we should take the man, even if it is going to be crowded." God reminds me that we are called to live not just for ourselves, but for others.

God turned a simple prompting into a life-changing moment.

Scriptures that Connect with this Story

Never walk away from someone who deserves help; your hand is God's hand for that person.
(Proverbs 3:27, NLT)

The true children of God are those who let God's Spirit lead them.
(Romans 8:14, ERV)

God consoles us as we endure the pain and hardship of life so that we may draw from His comfort and share it with others in their own struggles.
(2 Corinthians 1:4, NLT)

From My Story to Your Story

Here are some questions for you to answer:

1. As you read my story, what story from your own life came to mind? (Write it below)

2. How did God help you in your story?

3. What scripture connects with your story?

____

____

____

____

____

____

____

____

____

____

____

____

____

____

____

____

____

____

A Simple Prayer

God, I thank you for the gift of life
and for the miracles that come
through simple words and willing
hearts. Thank you for being at
work when we do not see
the full outcome right away.
Help us trust you every moment.
Amen.

Appendix Activities

Go to Appendix B and choose a few ways for "Practicing the Presence of God." Choose one app in the first section. Then choose one or two in the second section, "Paying Attention to God's Presence."
Do these practices as often as you can.
Share what you are experiencing with a friend and/or with the group you are in.

CHAPTER 4

Not Out of God's Sight

Today, I choose to look for God's miracles.

When my youngest was six weeks old, I finally felt ready to venture out. In the 1970s, double strollers didn't exist, so I held my two-year-old's hand while pushing the newborn in the stroller. I headed to the Denver mall, eager for a simple outing.

At the mall, I found my way to the clothing boutique. My two-and-a-half-year-old was fascinated by a circular rack of shirts, pants, and dresses and kept trying to step inside the ring of clothing. I gently pulled her back, not wanting her to disappear from my sight.

Suddenly, my newborn let out a piercing cry. I turned my attention toward her, instinctively checking to see what was wrong. In that moment, my two-year-old let go of my hand. When I looked back, she was gone.

I searched between the hanging clothes, certain that she had to be there, but she wasn't. Panic rose in my chest. How could a two-year-old disappear so quickly? My eyes darted between racks, searching for any glimpse of her.

I left the clothing store and stood looking out into the concourse. She could have gone anywhere with so many people. Standing in that crowded area, I whispered, *"God, please help me find her. Keep her safe."*

As I waited, I began to sense God saying, *"Start walking to the right."* I quickly glanced into each store along the way, hoping I might catch sight of her.

When I reached the far end of the mall, I noticed the JCPenney store. I felt God prompting me, "*Go into that store and see if she's there.*" I hurried toward it, pushing the stroller as fast as I could.

Inside, I found an employee and asked if she could make an announcement saying, *"We have a mother who is looking for a little girl named Shelley."* Not long after, an employee from the curtain department came up and said my daughter was with them.

As I walked to that area, I thanked God that she was safe and unharmed. When I reached her, she was sitting on the counter, happily jabbering with the employees. A wave of relief washed over me, instantly dissolving my fear.

One of the employees explained that she had seen my daughter running around, so she picked her up and placed her on the counter. When Shelley heard the announcement, "A mommy is looking for a little girl named Shelley," she pointed up toward the ceiling where the voice came from and said, "My name! My name!"

I thanked God for helping me find Shelley in such an enormous mall. I had my precious daughter back, safe in my arms. Even though I had lost sight of her, she was never out of God's Sight.

Ways God Helped Me in This Story

1. After we moved to Denver, several months passed and no monthly cycle was happening. I was upset because I longed for another child. Later I learned the high altitude had affected my body. The doctor gave me medicine, and my cycle returned. Soon I became pregnant, and on October 14, 1977, our little miracle arrived. I believe God used this delay so we would receive the precious daughter that God had planned for us.

2. In a crowded mall, it was easy to lose sight of my two-and-a-half-year-old little girl. But she was never 'Out of God's Sight'. He watched over her and kept her safe.

3. I had no idea where to find my daughter in that large mall. Yet God gently guided me and answered my desperate prayer in an amazing way.

God turned delay and fear into the precious gift He planned all along.

Scriptures that Connect with this Story

Therefore, I tell you, whatever you ask for in prayer, believe that you have received it, and it will be yours.
(Mark 11:24, NIV)

If you believe, you will receive whatever you ask in prayer.
(Matthew 21:22, NIV)

Some of the disciples, mistakenly thinking that Jesus wouldn't want to be bothered with the likes of children, began to rebuke the crowd. Let the little children come to Me; do not get in their way. For the kingdom of heaven belongs to children like these.
(Matthew 19:13b-14, Voice)

From My Story to Your Story

Here are some questions for you to answer:

1. When reading my story, what story of yours came to mind? (Write it below)
2. How did God help you in your story?
3. What scripture connects with your story?

____

____

____

____

____

____

____

____

____

____

____

____

____

____

____

____

____

____

A Simple Prayer

When we encounter concerns regarding our children, we will turn to you, God, and ask for your protection and guidance over their lives. Help us trust in your power and your love that never fails. Amen.

Appendix Activities

Go to Appendix B and choose a few ways for "Practicing the Presence of God." Choose one app in the first section. Then choose one or two in the second section, "Paying Attention to God's Presence."
Do these practices as often as you can.
Share what you are experiencing with a friend and/or with the group you are in.

CHAPTER 5

A Stranger at Our Table

Miracles grow…
where faith and perseverance meet.

I had been encouraging my husband to sell our white Buick Century, as it was costing us too much in repairs. He finally listed it in the Denver newspaper. Several people called, but no one seemed interested.

Then one day, a man called. He wanted to see the car, but he didn't have a way to get to us. He wondered if my husband could come pick him up.

My husband drove to the address given and invited the man to drive the Buick back to our home. When arriving, he agreed it was what he wanted and handed my husband $1,000 in cash.

As he started for the car, my husband said, "*Would you like to join us for lunch*?" The man hesitated, looking all around, but finally agreed and followed my husband into the house.

When he stepped inside, I noticed him scanning the room – the windows, the doors, the layout. The day was very warm, and I had closed all our windows and doors, so the AC would cool our house down. At the time, I thought he was just taking in an unfamiliar place.

My girls, aged one and three, were sitting in a highchair and a booster seat, ready to eat. My husband offered a prayer, thanking God for our food and for the new friend who was eating with us. When the prayer ended, I looked up and saw an interesting look on the man's face. Maybe he had never experienced a prayer spoken before a meal.

As we began to eat, the man kept looking around, listening to the conversation. Why did he seem edgy? He appeared to enjoy the meal and our little girls, yet something about being there unsettled him.

After he finished eating, he got into the Buick he had just purchased and drove away. After he drove away, life returned to normal. Two days later, we packed up the girls and headed to Oklahoma City to visit my sister--a trip we had been looking forward to for weeks.

It was wonderful to see my sister and family. In a short time, she invited us to sit down and eat a meal she had fixed. Several minutes into the meal, the phone rang. My sister answered it and then handed it to my husband with a puzzled look. It was a policeman.

The policeman asked if my husband was the owner of a white Buick. *"Yes, my husband said, I was the owner, but I sold it to a man two days ago."* The officer said that the plates were never put into the man's name, so they were still in my husband's name.

The policeman wanted to know what the man looked like and what he had told us. Then, he revealed the whole shocking story.

This man was wanted nationwide for armed robbery. He had robbed banks, convenience stores, gas stations—and he had a history of violence.

Knowing my husband had a thousand dollars in his pocket–from the purchase—could have easily tempted him to rob us. Why did he choose not to hurt us, even though he had us alone?

Maybe, just maybe, he saw something in us--something he had never experienced before. He had been welcomed into a home where God was honored, and people were treated with kindness. We had no idea who he really was, yet God did.

Though the truth was frightening, we were unharmed. God had protected us—not through fear, but through love lived out at an ordinary table. What remained was not terror, but awe. Once again, we had witnessed a miracle.

Ways God Helped Me in this Story

1. We invited the man who bought the car to have lunch with us. We did not know he was wanted nationwide for armed robbery, yet we welcomed him with kindness. In that moment, we showed him the love God had placed in our hearts.

2. The details that would build tension in hindsight was the man looking around, seeming edgy, the closed windows and doors, and the $1,000 in cash. He may have felt he was seeing something unexpected. God allowed our paths to cross so he could witness a family who loved Jesus.

3. When we later learned the truth, it was frightening, yet we were unharmed. God had protected us and gave this man a glimpse of Christ's love—perhaps, something he had never experienced before.

God turned danger into protection and testimony.

Scriptures that Connect with this Story

The Lord will keep you from all harm--
he will watch over your life.
(Psalm 121:7, NIV)

God doesn't miss a thing—
he's alert to good and evil alike.
(Proverbs 15:3, MSG)

Pray for God's help for them, for we are to
be kind to others, and God will bless us for it.
(1 Peter 3:9, TLB)

From My Story to Your Story

Here are some questions for you to answer:

1. As you read my story, what story from your own life came to mind? (Write it below)

2. How did God help you in your story?

3. What scripture connects with your story?

____

____

____

____

____

____

____

____

____

____

____

____

____

____

____

____

____

____

A Simple Prayer

God, thank you for watching over us
when we're unaware of danger
around us. Thank you for teaching
us to live out the love of Jesus, even
with strangers. Help us to trust you
in ordinary moments, knowing you
are always present.
Amen.

Appendix Activities

Go to Appendix B and choose a few ways for "Practicing the Presence of God." Choose one app in the first section. Then choose one or two in the second section, "Paying Attention to God's Presence."
Do these practices as often as you can.
Share what you are experiencing with a friend and/or with the group you are in.

CHAPTER 6

A Seat Across the Aisle

We will only understand the miracle
of life fully when we allow the
unexpected to happen.
Paulo Coelho

As I boarded my flight to Florida, I silently asked God to place me near someone I could help. Southwest allowed passengers to choose their own seats, so I waited for His nudge.

I sensed a gentle pull toward a seat on the left side of the plane. I didn't know why—I just followed. When I sat down, I noticed a woman across the aisle, and after takeoff we struck up a conversation that lasted the entire flight.

She shared about her experiences in the military, and I spoke about my years as a seminary professor. I was also able to share how God turned my deepest challenges into blessings. She was fascinated by how I trusted God, even after my husband left to begin a new life with someone else. She listened intently, yet I had no idea how the talk had deeply moved her.

I decided to offer her my email address before exiting the plane, though I doubted I'd ever hear from her again. To my delight, she sent an email a week later.

She told me she had lost the paper with my email but found it again–and she couldn't stop thinking about our conversation. She said she never talks to anyone on flights and has never met anyone like me. She wanted to understand how--and why—I was so different. Something about that conversation had unsettled her in the best way.

A year later, the military transferred her to a city just three hours from me allowing us to visit each other. I invited her to read the Bible every Tuesday, talking about what she thought as she read it. She began to see things in a very different way and was open to learning about God.

Over time she decided to become a Christian, attend church, and to find how to grow in different ways.

What began as a simple prayer—to place me near someone I could help—became a friendship, a spiritual journey, and a life transformed. God did not waste a seat assignment. His miracle came as an Unexpected Meeting on a plane.

Ways God Helped Me in This Story

1. I was thankful that I had prayed about the seat God wanted me to have on the plane. He knew the person He wanted me to help.

2. I usually did not give my email address, but that day I felt led to share it. Even though she misplaced it at first, she later found it—without realizing God had guided her. That simple email began our friendship.

3. I asked Sonya if she would like to join me for a Bible study on Tuesdays, like the ones I encouraged my students to attend. She said yes. Through that time together, she began to desire a relationship with Christ and to attend church again, after many years.

4. Later Sonya told me I was unlike anyone she had ever met. I believe she was seeing the difference that comes from spending time with Jesus.

God turned a simple plane seat into a divine appointment.

Scriptures that Connect with this Story

With Jesus' help we will continually offer
our sacrifice of praise to God by
telling others of the glory of his name.
(Hebrews 13:15, TLB)

If someone asks about your hope as
a believer, always be ready to
explain it. But do this in a
gentle and respectful way.
(1 Peter 3:15, NLT)

So, we have been sent to speak for
Christ. It is like God is calling
to people through us.
(2 Corinthians 5:20, ERV)

From My Story to Your Story

Here are some questions for you to answer:

1. As you read my story, what story from your own life came to mind? (Write it below)

2. How did God help you in your story?

3. What scripture connects with your story?

A Simple Prayer

God, I want to thank you for placing
people in our paths at just the right time.
Thank you for reminding us that no meeting
is accidental when you are involved.
Help us to be willing, available, and
faithful to your nudges in any
unexpected conversation. Use our
words, our stories, and our lives
to reflect your love to others.
Amen.

Appendix Activities

Go to Appendix B and choose a few ways for "Practicing the Presence of God." Choose one app in the first section. Then choose one or two in the second section, "Paying Attention to God's Presence."

Do these practices as often as you can.

Share what you are experiencing with a friend and/or with the group you are in.

CHAPTER 7

The Day Fear Met Faith

I believe God is still writing miracles into my story.

On September 9, 2023, my husband and I moved to the Florida Panhandle to be near our youngest daughter. I thought I was starting a new chapter in life. I had no idea how true that would be—or how difficult the next year would become.

Some years before, my body had been sending signals—gluten issues in 2012, a serious parasite in 2015, word-finding difficulties in 2020. But nothing prepared me for what came next.

In July of 2024, painful spasms began in my back. Tests showed a compression fracture at T10 in my spine. The pain was so severe that I slept in a recliner for weeks.

Four weeks later, I had surgery. During the procedure, the doctor noticed something unusual in the bone dust from my spine and sent it for testing. A week later, a nurse gently told me the results: I had multiple myeloma, a cancer of white blood cells found in bone marrow. The fracture had happened because the cancer cells had broken up my bone.

I was shocked. I had tried to exercise, walk often, and eat healthy food. How could this happen?

The oncologist, Dr. Hassan, recommended chemotherapy with many pills, along with treatments. I told him I would think about it.

A few days later, he asked me to return so he could share some more information. He explained that 80% of my bone marrow showed cancer.

I prayed quietly, asking God, "What should I do"? In my heart, I sensed Him saying, "Gwen, follow the doctor's advice." A warm, comforting presence washed over me, and I felt a quiet assurance that I was not alone.

On October 25, 2024, I began chemotherapy. As I sat in the waiting room, fear started to overwhelm me. I sensed God's voice saying, "Don't focus on yourself, just encourage others who are here." From that day on, whenever I entered the oncology area, I prayed that God would lead me to someone who needed encouragement.

A year later, I sat in Dr. Hassan's office to hear new test results. When he walked in, I could tell by his face that something had changed. He said, "You have gone from 80% to less than 5% cancer in your bone marrow. It could be four, three, two or even one percent--because doctors rarely record zero.

I told him, "I believe God has done a miracle." He was not a Christian, but even he knew something remarkable had happened.

Because of my improvement, I was allowed to stop taking the medications, though I continue monthly checkups and a needle injection to keep any remaining cancer under control.

Every day, I thank God for the miracle He has done and for the strength He continues to give me.

Ways God Helped Me in This Story

1. If the T10 compression fracture had not occurred, the cancer in my bone marrow might not have been discovered until it was far more advanced. The four-week wait for the surgery was the worst pain I have ever experienced. Yet God already knew the doctor who would perform the procedure and test the bone fragments, revealing what needed to be found. What felt unbearable became life-saving.

2. During chemotherapy, God has given me unexpected opportunities to encourage others who are also fighting cancer. I pray for them and speak hope into their struggle. In helping them, I often forget my own pain and am reminded that God can use me even here.

3. I continue to face challenges from the past, including digestive issues. Yet God has provided a doctor who is helping me care for my gut. I trust the future because it is in God's hands. God turned unbearable pain into life-saving grace and the suffering into a new ministry.

Scriptures that Connect with this Story

He was pierced for our transgressions,
he was crushed for our iniquities,
the punishment that brought us peace was
on him, and by His wounds, we are healed.
(Isaiah 53:5, NIV)

If you depend on God, your body and mind will
be free… and will experience healing and health.
(Proverbs 3:8, Voice)

I will restore you to health and
heal your wounds, declares the Lord.
(Jeremiah 30:17, NIV)

From My Story to Your Story

Here are some questions for you to answer:

1. As you read my story, what story from your own life came to mind? (Write it below)

2. How did God help you in your story?

3. What bible verse comes to mind when you think about your story?

A Simple Prayer

God, when illness enters our lives,
help us to trust You. Use our weakness
to comfort others, our fear to grow
faith, and our pain to show your love.
Thank you for walking with us through
illness and for the miracles—seen
and unseen—you give each day.
Amen.

Appendix Activities

1. Take the "Self-Reflection Tool" again in Appendix A.
2. Discuss: How have you grown by remembering miracles in your life? And how have you grown in "Practicing the Presence of God"?
3. Where do you still want to grow?

APPENDIX A

Where Is God Growing You?

You may have experienced some of the emotions I went through in my stories. For instance:

- I would be afraid I'd get hurt when I saw a person coming toward me on a sidewalk.

- If my car broke down in a troubled neighborhood, I would be afraid someone would hurt me.

- I'm afraid someone would steal our car, which was for sale, if we let them drive it alone.

- I'm not sure a stranger who offered us a ride would be safe.

- If my child disappeared in a mall, I would be afraid someone might hurt her.

- If a person buys something from us, I would be afraid to invite them to eat with us.

- If someone had an accident on the side of the road, I would hope I could help them.

- I was shocked and afraid when I found out I had a serious illness—cancer.

God can help us replace our feelings of fear, anger, sadness, and worry with positive feelings like faith, love, peace, and joy.

Self-Reflection Tool

Put a number in each question below to see where you've been growing or may need to grow. Then add the numbers in the TOTAL section.

Rate yourself using this scale:

0 – Never 1 – Sometimes 2 – Regularly

1) **FEELING SAFE** (Add the TOTAL: ______)

Proverbs 18:10 - *"The name of the LORD is a fortified tower; the righteous run to it and are **safe**."*

Psalm 4:8 - *"God is **our shelter and our strength**. When troubles seem near, God is nearer, and He's ready to help"*

_____ **Free from hurt** (Do you go to God for help when someone ***hurts*** you?)

_____ **Safe** (Since God is your refuge, do you go to him when you feel ***unsafe***?)

_____ **Protected** (When you begin worrying about what might happen, do you remember that God ***protects*** you?)

_____ **Emotional Safety** (Do you feel ***safe*** to pour out your heart to God whenever you feel anxious, sad, or lonely?)

2) FEELING FEARLESS (Add the TOTAL: ______)

Psalm 27:1 – *"The LORD is my light and my salvation – whom shall I* ***fear****? The Lord is the stronghold of my life – of whom shall I be* ***afraid****?"*

Isaiah 41:10 – *"So do not* ***fear,*** *for I am with you; do not be dismayed, for I am your God. I will strengthen you and help you."*

_____ **Courageous** (When faced with a challenge, do you ask God for the grace to respond with ***courage and love***?)

_____ **Unafraid** (When something in your life is making you afraid, can you shift your focus back to God so that you can remain ***unafraid and calm***?)

_____ **Fearless** (Do you find strength to be ***fearless*** by remembering how faithful God has been in the past?)

_____ **Boldness** (When you want to do something that feels difficult, can you trust God to fill you with ***boldness***?)

3) FEELING PEACEFUL (Add the TOTAL: ______)

Psalm 37:7 – *"Be* ***still*** *before the Lord and wait patiently for him."*

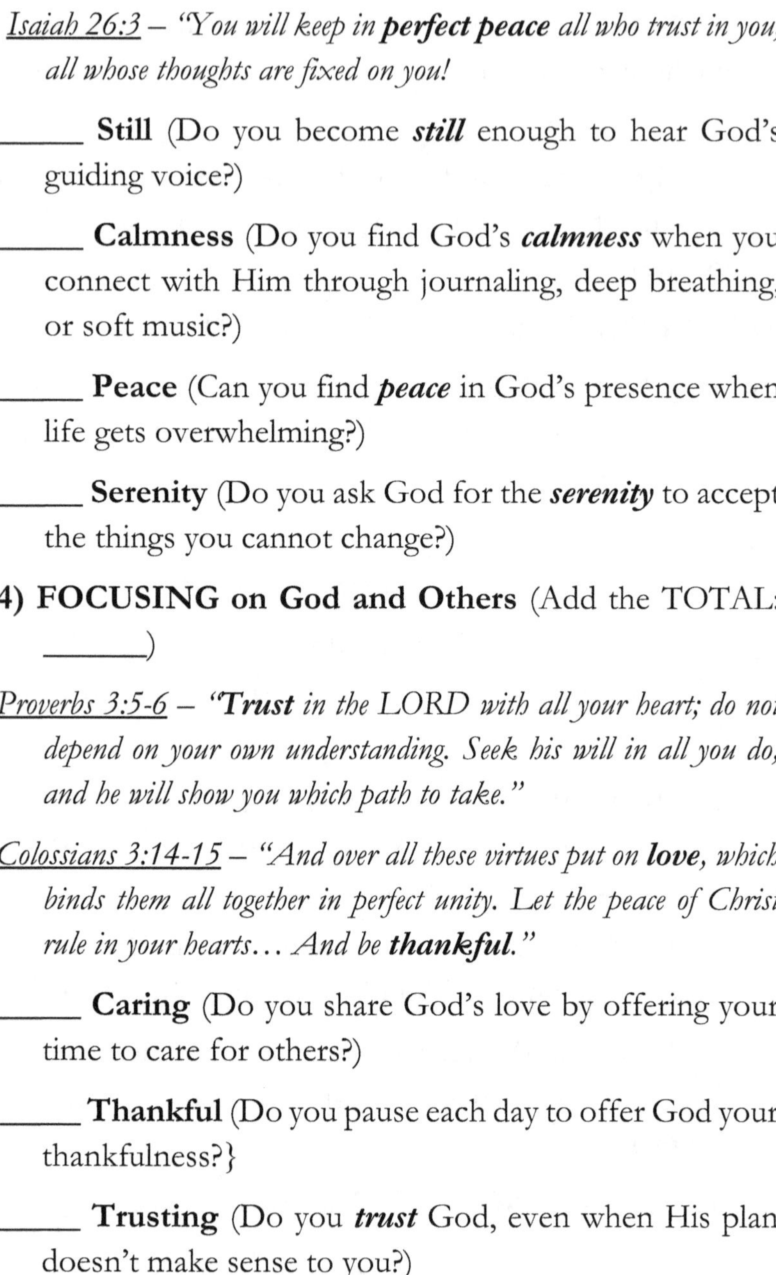

Isaiah 26:3 – *"You will keep in **perfect peace** all who trust in you, all whose thoughts are fixed on you!*

_____ **Still** (Do you become ***still*** enough to hear God's guiding voice?)

_____ **Calmness** (Do you find God's ***calmness*** when you connect with Him through journaling, deep breathing, or soft music?)

_____ **Peace** (Can you find ***peace*** in God's presence when life gets overwhelming?)

_____ **Serenity** (Do you ask God for the ***serenity*** to accept the things you cannot change?)

4) FOCUSING on God and Others (Add the TOTAL: ______)

Proverbs 3:5-6 – *"**Trust** in the LORD with all your heart; do not depend on your own understanding. Seek his will in all you do, and he will show you which path to take."*

Colossians 3:14-15 – *"And over all these virtues put on **love**, which binds them all together in perfect unity. Let the peace of Christ rule in your hearts… And be **thankful**."*

_____ **Caring** (Do you share God's love by offering your time to care for others?)

_____ **Thankful** (Do you pause each day to offer God your thankfulness?}

_____ **Trusting** (Do you ***trust*** God, even when His plan doesn't make sense to you?)

_____ **Loving** (Is your ***love*** for God transforming the way you treat others?)

Lord, thank You for the ways You are already working in my life. Continue to strengthen the areas where I am growing and gently guide me in the places where I need You most. Amen.

APPENDIX B

Ways to Practice the Presence of God

What does it mean to practice God's presence? Brother Lawrence describes it as *'habitual, silent, and a secret conversation with God.'* It is like a personal relationship.

Learning to have a "quiet time" with God helps avoid the busyness of life. Practicing God's presence is maintaining a continual awareness of Him throughout your daily life.

We can do this by talking to God (prayer), listening to God (silence or scripture), or finding ways to keep our minds on him.

A. FIRST, you can spend time with God through **apps** that can help you:

1. "Holy Bible" app (that has a red color): You can pick a Chronological Reading Plan, a One-Year Bible Plan, a New Testament Plan, the Gospels Plan, etc.

2. "Soulspace" app: It only lasts 5-7 minutes but is focused every day on a different bible verse and ways to grow spiritually and emotionally.

3. "Pause" app: John Eldredge has put this together. It has helped me grow spiritually and emotionally. He has two Programs, "Experience Jesus" and "30 Days to Resilient" *(I've gone through both programs several times because it is so helpful.)*

4. "Lectio 365" app: It is a daily devotional resource with scriptures, prayers, and a Morning and Night devotional.

5. "Breathwrk" app: This can help calm the nervous system, release stress, help our lungs, and shift our minds from "fight-or-flight" to relaxation.

6. "Tapping Solution" app: This is a stress-relief procedure, known as an EFT (Emotional Freedom Techniques). It involves physical tapping with your fingertips as you focus on a specific stressor. Some of the choices are: Anxiety, Fear, Anger, Stress, Sleep, and more. *(One day, I was in a lot of physical pain. I chose a tapping session to ease this pain. When I chose the level of my pain (0 to 10) it was nine. At the end, my pain was three. The tapping had helped lower my pain.)*

B. SECOND, there are some practical ways to spend time in the Presence of God. Miracles often happen when we are Paying Attention to God's Presence.

1. Collect pocket-sized pictures of Jesus as a reminder to think about Him. You can also put pictures of Jesus around your house in any room. I have a picture of Jesus with these words: "I love you more than you can ever know."
2. During the day, you might whisper, "Fill me with your peace, Jesus." Or you might spend the time in silence. Psalm 46:10 (NKJV) says, "Be still and know that I am God."
3. When you lie down at night, hug a pillow as if you were hugging God. Then say, "I love you, God." Make God your final thought before you fall asleep.
4. Place a picture of Jesus, a Bible, or a cross next to your bed, so you can see it when you lie down.
5. When in nature, look at each lovely thing and thank God for the creation He made.
6. Keep an empty chair for Jesus at your table or anywhere in your house. Consider Jesus being there and connect and whisper something to Him.
7. Pray the Attributes of God (in Appendix C) to feel closer to God and to thank Him for his goodness.
8. Thankfulness connects us to God as we shift our focus from our struggles to His goodness. Thanking God at night or in the morning will keep you close to God. Psalm 100:4 (NIV) says, "Enter his gates with thanksgiving and his courts with praise; give thanks to him and praise his name."
9. You can use scriptures to pray. One example is the "Lord's Prayer" (Matthew 6:9-13). You can also insert your name in the verse you are praying.

10. Singing, humming, or playing a song can help you connect with God. If you are upset or frustrated, play a soft song that gives you thoughts about God.
11. If God has done a miracle or answered your prayer, use a jar and a piece of paper to write down what happened. If you begin to feel anxious or sad one day, read something from that jar. It will help you return to God's presence.
12. When you see a person who looks sad, upset, or frustrated, say a silent prayer for them. If you find out someone has health issues, pray for them as well.
13. When you are sick, continue connecting with Jesus to produce the best mental state for a rapid recovery.
14. When you are facing fear or spiritual battles, call upon God to hold you in his arms and take you to his shelter. Ask him to have angels around you for safety. Deuteronomy 33:27 (Voice) says, "The eternal God is your shelter; He holds you up in His everlasting arms."
15. Whisper to God throughout the day about even the smallest matter. He loves to help you with anything.
16. Instead of talking to yourself, talk to Jesus. He will help you with what you are thinking.
17. As you go about your day, keep whispering: "Lord, put your thoughts in my mind."
18. Imagine yourself in the presence of Jesus (sitting next to him or in his arms) and talk to him.
19. Once a month, my daughter and I spend a Saturday with what we call "Time with Jesus."

We are journaling together about three things. First, we write a short 'Brain Dump" to clear out our minds and hearts so we can connect with God. Second, we ask God, "What do you want to say to me right now?" Third, we ask God, "What should I do during these five hours alone with you?" Then my daughter and I share what we have written down. We then spend five hours by ourselves.

Here are a few things I have chosen to do: praying or a prayer walk, being still, singing or finding some sacred music to listen to, reading the Scriptures, doing artistic work with a Scripture that touches you, or spending time listening to Jesus.

In the late afternoon, my daughter and I get back together and share the experiences we have had with Jesus that day.

20. Who do you think has spent the most time with God? Jesus! He frequently withdrew from the crowd to pray, he took time to recharge, and he spent private time finding out what God wanted him to do. He was a great model for a life of intimate prayer, as he sought guidance from the Father before making decisions. An example is in Luke 7:12-13 (NIV), "Jesus went out to a mountainside to pray, and spent the night praying to God. When morning came, he called his disciples to him and chose twelve of them."

Come near to God and
he will come near to you.
(James 4:8, NIV)

APPENDIX C

Attributes for Closeness with God

One way you can draw closer to God is by using the alphabet to reflect on God's attributes. You can pray these in bed or during your regular prayer time, thanking God for his goodness.

Look below, and you will see a scripture after each alphabetical word. If you see a version (like NIV, etc.) after the scripture, use it because very few versions are available.

When there is nothing after the scripture, you can choose a version you want (NIV, NLT, NKJV, AMP, CSB, etc.) This experience gives you a chance to know more about God's attributes.

A. Awesome (Psalm 145:3-6, NIV)
   Advocate (I John 2:1)
   Author (Hebrews 12:2, NKJV)

B. Bountiful (Psalm 65:11, NLT)
   Bread of Life (John 6:35)
   Bridegroom (Matthew 9:15)

C. Creator (Genesis 1:1)
Comforter (II Corinthians 1:3-4)
Compassionate (Psalm 103:13, NLT)

D. Deliverer (Psalm 18:2)
Dwelling Place (Psalm 90:1)
Defender (Proverbs 23:11, NLT)

E. El Shaddai (Genesis 17:1, NLT)
Emmanuel (Matthew 1:23)
Eternal (Deuteronomy 33:27)

F. Father (Matthew 6:9)
Forgiving (Daniel 9:9)
Friend (John 15:15)

G. Good Shepherd (John 10:11)
Glorious (Exodus 15:11, NKJV)
Gracious (Psalm 145:8)

H. Holy, Holy, Holy (Isaiah 6:3)
Hope (Romans 15:13)
Hiding Place (Psalm 32:7)

I. Immortal (I Timothy 1:17)
Infinite (Psalm 147:5, NKJV)
I Am (Exodus 3:14)

J. Just (Deuteronomy 32:4)
Jehovah Jireh/Lord will provide (Genesis 22:14)
Judge (Psalm 75:7)

K. King of Kings (Revelation 19:16)
Kindness (Ephesians 2:7)
Knowable/Knows (I John 3:20)

L. Lamb of God (John 1:29)
Life (John 14:6)
Lord of Lords (I Timothy 6:15)

M. Merciful (Luke 6:36, NIV)
Miracle Maker (Psalm 77:14, NIV)
Majestic (Psalm 8:1)

N. Never Fail (Lamentations 3:22-23, AMP)
Noble (Psalm 16:3, CSB)
Name above all Names (Philippians 2:9, NLT)

O. Our Righteousness (Jeremiah 23:6, NLT)
One God (Ephesians 4:4-6)
O God (Psalm 63:1, NLT)

P. Patience (I Timothy 1:15-16, NLT)
Prince of Peace (Isaiah 9:6)
Potter (Isaiah 64:8)

Q. Quencher of Thirst (John 4:14, MSG)
Quieter of Storms (Mark 4:39, NIV)
Qualified (Colossians 1:12, NKJV)

R. Refuge (Psalm 46:1)
Righteous (Psalm 145:17)
Resurrection and Life (John 11:25)

S. Savior (Luke 2:11)
Shepherd (Psalm 23:1)
Shelter (Psalm 91:1-2)

T. Triumphant (Colossians 2:15, NKJV)
Truth (John 14:6)
Teacher (John 13:13)

U. Unsearchable (Romans 11:33, NIV)
Understandable (Psalm 147:5)
Upright (Deuteronomy 32:4)

V. Vine (John 15:5)
Victorious (I Corinthians 15:57)
Very Present Help (Psalm 46:1, NKJV)

W. Wonderful Counselor (Isaiah 9:6)
Word (John 1:1)
Way (John 14:6)

X. Examine/EXaminer of Hearts (Psalm 139:23-24, NLT)
Xristos/Greek language for Christ (Matthew 16:16, ESV)
Xenodochos – Greek language for hospitality (I Timothy 5:10, NIV)

Y. Yahweh /I Am Who I Am (Exodus 3:14)
Yahweh Nissi/the Lord is my Banner (Exodus 17:15, NLT)
Yes and Amen (II Corinthians 1:20, ESV)

Z. Zealous/Zeal (Isaiah 9:7, NKJV)
Zion's King (Psalm 2:6, NIV)
Zenith/Fill with His Glory (Psalm 72:19)

APPENDIX D

Group Leader's Guide

1. Opening (2–3 minutes)

- Welcome the group
- Open with a short prayer, asking God to guide the time and make it safe for sharing
- Remind the group that what we share stays here

"Lord, thank You for bringing us together. Help us notice Your presence as we listen and reflect. Amen."

---

2. Read the Chapter (3-5 Minutes)

- Read the chapter aloud
- You may read it or ask someone else to read

---

3. Quiet Reflection (about 5 minutes)

- Have them turn to: "From My Story to Your Story" and have every person spend time personally answering the three questions

---

4. Group Discussion (10–20 minutes)

- Have them discuss the responses they wrote down from, "My Story to Your Story." Then have them share the answer to questions two and three.

---

5. Discussion about additional things from Appendix A, B, & C (10–15 minutes)

- Have them discuss 'Self-Reflection Tool" AND "Practicing the Presence of God."

- On the final week, have them go to the Self-Reflection Tool and take it again at home. Have them share how it has felt to talk about their miracles, how to experience Practicing the Presence of God, and deciding where they want to grow more now.

---

6. Closing Prayer (2–3 minutes)

- Close with a prayer at the end of the time together (or invite someone else to pray).

- On the last week, end with "My Final Words" and a prayer.

Leader reminders:

- Sharing is always voluntary
- There are no right or wrong answers
- Listening is as important as speaking
- Your role is not really to teach, correct, or explain. God does the real work. Trust Him.

My Final Words

As you close this book, my prayer is
that you have noticed the
miracle moments in your own life.

Sometimes God's presence
appears in dramatic ways.
But more often, His miracles unfold
quietly—in an unexpected situation,
an answer to prayer, or the
strength to face another day.

These moments may seem small
at first. Yet when we look back, we
can see that God was there all along,
guiding, protecting, and loving us.

May your eyes always be open to the
miracle moments that surround you.

Miracles are often God's presence
in the ordinary moments of our lives.

Other Books by Gwen Ebner

Intimate Moments with the Father: Connecting with God in Mind and Heart

Peace in Anxious Times: A Holistic Approach

Broken by Accident: Finding Purpose in Your Stories

Scan the QR code to order!

www.ingramcontent.com/pod-product-compliance
Lightning Source LLC
LaVergne TN
LVHW010841120826
845149LV00020B/3422